What Do You Like to Draw?

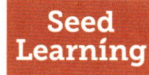

What do you like to draw?

I like to draw
a snowman.

I like to draw
a white snowman.

What do you like to draw?

I like to draw a deer.

I like to draw
a yellow deer.

What do you like to draw?

I like to draw a whale.

I like to draw
a gray whale.

What do you like to draw?

I like to draw an octopus.

I like to draw
a purple octopus.

What do you like to draw?

I like to draw a shark.

I like to draw
a brown shark.

What do you like to draw?

I like to draw a fox.

I like to draw
an orange fox.

What do you like to draw?

I like to draw mountains.

I like to draw
pink mountains.

Let's learn more about Yom Kippur.

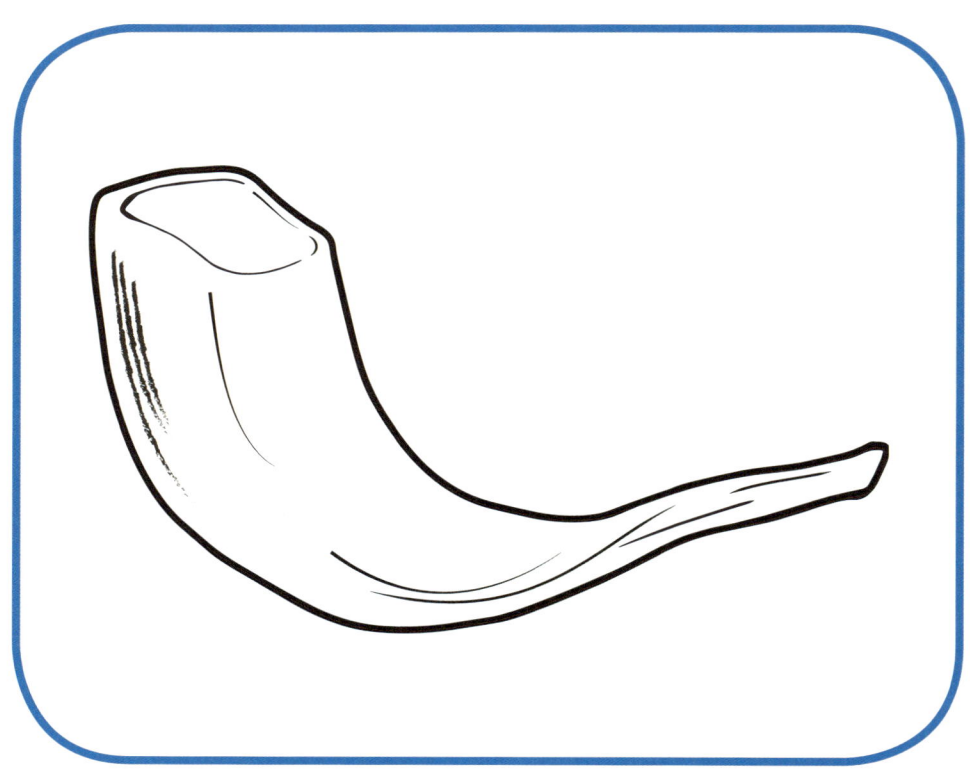

Color the shofar.